THE DAY
THE NUMBERS

LEONARD SIMON

Junior High School Curriculum Co-ordinator
Board of Education, City of New York

JEANNE BENDICK

pictures by Jeanne Bendick

Whittlesey House · *McGraw-Hill*
McGRAW-HILL BOOK COMPANY, INC.
NEW YORK · TORONTO · LONDON

DISAPPEARED

To Shirley and Stephen and Ann Simon

3-4

With many thanks to Julius Schwartz for looking at the
original manuscript and making suggestions and for his
continuous encouragement.

THE DAY THE NUMBERS DISAPPEARED
Copyright © 1963 by Leonard Simon and Jeanne Bendick.
All rights reserved. Printed in the United States of America.
This book or parts thereof may not be reproduced in any form
without written permission of the publishers.
Library of Congress Catalog Card Number: 62-21573
Published by Whittlesey House,
     a division of the McGraw-Hill Book Company, Inc.

The whole class loved Mr. Dibbs.

They could hardly wait to get to school in the morning, it was such fun having him for a teacher. And when they got home, they were popping with things they had learned from Mr. Dibbs.

Mr. Dibbs said he learned things from them, too. "You'd be surprised," he said, "how many things I learn from this class."

Mr. Dibbs and the class were so pleased with each other that *THE FIGHT* came as a surprise to everybody. The fight was over arithmetic. It started when Mr. Dibbs was writing the arithmetic lesson on the board. He distinctly heard three groans and four sighs. He put down the chalk and turned around.

"And what is the matter with arithmetic?" he asked.

Steve sighed. "I guess I just don't like arithmetic, Mr. Dibbs. In fact, I don't like numbers. I wish we didn't have any."

"They're dull," said Cathy.

"Who needs them?" David asked.

Mr. Dibbs looked thoughtfully around the class. "Well," he said. "Does everybody feel that way?"

"You *bet!*" shouted four more pupils at the same time.

Mr. Dibbs sat on a corner of his desk and whistled quietly to himself for a minute. "It's hard for me to understand," he said, "because I *love* numbers. I like number marks, and the things you can do with them. I like arithmetic. But of course, everyone to his own taste, as the old lady said, kissing the cow."

The class giggled.

"Do you really think," Mr. Dibbs asked, "that things would be easier without numbers and the marks for them?"

Everybody nodded.

"Are you prepared to defend your belief in a fair fight?" Mr. Dibbs asked solemnly. "Are you prepared to prove to me that arithmetic is only a nuisance? Because if you are, we'll start tomorrow. No numbers, and no arithmetic."

The class cheered.

"Just a minute," Mr. Dibbs interrupted. "If you lose the fight, you have to pay the penalty."

"What's the penalty?" David asked cautiously.

"Who cares?" Steve grinned. "No numbers and no arithmetic tomorrow! What a break!"

When the class came in the next morning, Mr. Dibbs was already working at his desk. "I've been here quite a while," he said, looking up. "Why shouldn't I mark you all late?"

"Late!" They looked at the clock, but it was blank. Somebody had covered the face, and all the number marks were gone. They couldn't tell whether they were late or not!

Mr. Dibbs looked like a boy on his way to the circus.

"Larry, you may take the milk orders," he said.

Larry stood up. "Everyone who wants milk today, raise your hand . . ." he started, but Mr. Dibbs interrupted.

"What are you doing?" he asked in an interested voice.

"Why, I'm counting the number . . ." Larry began.

"Counting?" said Mr. Dibbs. "What's that? There's no such thing as counting. You'll just have to write down all the names, and when you go to pick up the milk, you'll have to match a milk carton to each name. That's what people did before they had numbers."

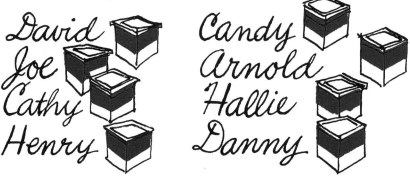

David
Joe
Cathy
Henry

Candy
Arnold
Hallie
Danny

"That will take *forever*," Larry wailed.

"Oh, well," said Mr. Dibbs calmly. "It doesn't matter, because time doesn't mean anything to you now."

"All right," Larry sighed. "Those who want milk, put the money on your desk."

"How are you going to count it or figure out change without using numbers?" Mr. Dibbs asked interestedly.

The class looked at each other. "Maybe we could charge it," Hallie said hopefully.

· "Looks as if we'll have to skip milk this morning," said Mr. Dibbs regretfully. "But it's almost time for the science television lesson anyway. Danny, will you turn on the set, please?"

"I forget," Danny said. "Is it Channel Eleven or Channel Thirteen?"

"Just turn the dial until you come to the right channel," somebody suggested.

They missed the beginning of the science lesson.

After it was over, the class had to finish the invitations they were writing to their parents to visit school. Mr. Dibbs walked around the class, watching, as they started to address the envelopes.

"What are you doing there, friend Ralph?" he asked suddenly.

"I'm writing my home address on the envelope."

Mr. Dibbs shook his head. "But don't you remember, you can't use any number marks today."

Ralph looked confused. "But how can you address an envelope without them?"

"Don't ask *me!*" said Mr. Dibbs. "Let's see what you can figure out."

When it seemed about time for the class to read, he told them to turn to the page where they had left off yesterday.

"What page was it?" Lisa asked.

Everybody looked at Mr. Dibbs and Mr. Dibbs looked at the ceiling. "How can I tell you? Just turn the pages until you find it."

The recess bell rang after reading, and the class shouted for punch ball. "It's all right with me," Mr. Dibbs said, "but it's going to be pretty dull if you can't keep score. How will you know who won?"

After some argument they decided that when anybody scored he would go and stand on his side of home base. This worked fine until there weren't enough people left to play.

"Well, it was getting too hot anyway," said David, as they came back into the classroom. "I wonder how hot it is." He looked at the thermometer. "Uh, oh," he said. The number marks weren't there. Somebody had put tape over them.

"Maybe you only *think* you're hot," Mr. Dibbs said cheerfully. "But you certainly can't prove it. The thermometer is just a *little* thing, but think what it would be like if all the number marks in the world, or even in this town, disappeared!

"Suppose you went into Mr. Mark's shoe store—how could he tell what size you wear? He'd just have to keep taking out boxes and boxes until he found a pair of shoes that fit!

"How would they know how many gallons of gas to put in your car at the gas station?

"How could you pay for anything at the supermarket?

"With no number marks on the dial, how could you call each other on the phone?

"And can you even imagine trying to build a house without being able to measure anything?"

At lunch time, the class had a meeting and decided to ask Mr. Dibbs to let them use numbers again. Life was getting too complicated without them.

"The winner of a fair fight!" he said, shaking hands with himself over his head. "But don't forget," he said severely, "you have to pay the penalty. The penalty is——" He tried to look as if he were deciding, but the class knew he had decided it long ago.

"The penalty is that you'll have to earn the numbers back. You'll have to work your way toward the numbers we use today the way people did in history."

"Great!" everybody shouted. "That sounds like fun!"

"Well, let's say an interesting experiment," Mr. Dibbs said. "A very long time ago, if you wanted to tell how many people you saw, you might say,

"As many as there are suns. (How many would you mean?)

"As many as the wings of a bird.   (How many would you mean?)

"As many as the leaves on a clover.

"As many as the legs on a dog.

"As many as the fingers on one hand.

"Who can tell me what day of the month this is, without numbers?"

Jeff said, "As many days have gone by as I have fingers on both hands."

Mr. Dibbs nodded.   "In almost the beginning of counting," he told them, "people saw that it was easier to use their fingers to show how many than to point to a bird or a flower or a dog.   So they used fingers for counting."

"Maybe we could manage with just fingers," said Cathy hopefully.

14

But when the class tried, they found that there were not enough fingers for most things. And how could you divide or multiply fingers?

Today is April ?   Room ?
Present ?
Absent ?
Assembly at ? o'clock

"Maybe we could use marks," Arnold said thoughtfully. "We should have used marks keeping score, instead of people. Marks aren't like people or fingers. You can make as many marks as you need."

"Thousands of years ago," Mr. Dibbs explained, "the Egyptians had a number system that used marks. They used strokes like this:

OUR NUMBER WORDS   EGYPTIAN NUMBER MARKS

one |
two ||
three |||
four ||||
five |||||

"Just for fun, let's suppose we are all Egyptians. How would you write

six ⟶

From here on, you will find many questions in this book. Answer first, then follow the arrow, (turn the book sideways) to check your answer. ⟶

Strokes are fine for small numbers, but would you like to write eighty?
six hundred and fifty seven?
one hundred thousand?
using strokes!

"The Egyptians didn't like it either, so they invented a new mark to use when they came to ten.

"Now their system looked like this

OUR NUMBER WORDS	EGYPTIAN NUMBER MARKS
one	I
two	II
and all the strokes to nine	IIIIIIIII
Then ten	∩
How did they write eleven?	∩I

How do you think they wrote

twelve

How do you think they wrote

twenty

"Have you figured out," Mr. Dibbs asked, "the plan the Egyptians used to write these numbers? Try writing

seventy five

Danny said, "The Egyptians kept repeating their symbols when they wrote the numbers."

"Right!" said Mr. Dibbs. "But there was something even more important to their plan."

"I know," said Laurie, running to the blackboard.

"Right!" said Mr. Dibbs again. "Now who else sees what plan they used?"

They all shouted, ADDITION!

They used addition!"

What numbers do you think these symbols show?

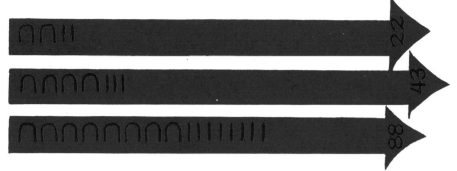

∩∩|| → 22

∩∩∩∩||| → 43

∩∩∩∩∩∩∩∩|||||||| → 88

"I'd hate to have to write a thousand that way," David groaned. "And a million would take all day!"

"Well, the Egyptians figured out something special for ten," Mr. Dibbs reminded him. "What do you think they did for a hundred?"

"They invented a new mark!"

"Right!" Mr. Dibbs grinned. "They used a mark that looked like a coiled rope." @

"I bet I could write a hundred and two the way the Egyptians did," Lisa said.

How would you write   a hundred and forty six   ∩∩∩∩|||||

five hundred and twenty   @@@@@∩∩

What numbers were the Egyptians thinking of when they wrote

"Now does everyone see," Mr. Dibbs asked, "what three ideas the Egyptians used?"

Joe said, "They used a stroke for one,
an arch for ten,
a coil for a hundred,
and I'll bet they had other symbols for a thousand
and ten thousand
and maybe even more."

1000

Steve said, "And they repeated the symbols, but I think most important was that they used addition. Why don't people still use the Egyptian number marks?"

"Wouldn't it be hard to get such long numbers on a ruler?" Nancy asked.

"Let's try some arithmetic with the Egyptian number marks," Mr. Dibbs said.

"Let's add

"That's not hard," Larry said.
"Maybe not, but now try this one.

And this one? It's even harder."

"This system is easier than what we do now," David said. "I wouldn't miss our number marks at all."

"It does look easier," Mr. Dibbs agreed. "Let's try some subtraction with it."

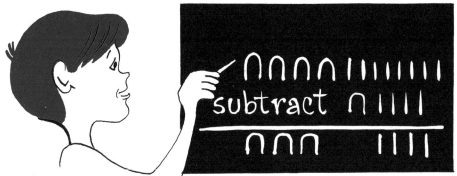

"Just as easy as addition! Now try

$$\text{subtract } \text{ⓒⓒⓒ} \cap\cap |||||| \text{ (ⓒⓒ⊓ ||)}$$

And can you do this one?"

$$\text{subtract } \cap\cap\cap\cap || \text{ } \cap ||||||| \text{ (|||||)}$$

"That was harder, because you had to exchange one arch for ten strokes, but not *too* hard," Joe said after a minute.

"It's *still* easy," Steve said.

"All right, Steve," Mr. Dibbs said softly. "Now let's multiply."

$$\text{ⓒⓒⓒⓒ} \cap\cap\cap || \times \text{ⓒⓒ} \cap\cap\cap\cap |||||$$

"Or maybe you'd rather try dividing, Steve." Mr. Dibbs grinned.

$$\cap\cap ||||) \text{ⓒⓒ} \cap\cap\cap\cap |||$$

"Well, Mr. Dibbs," Steve sighed at last. "It looks like the Egyptians could count, add and subtract easily enough, but they must have had an awful time multiplying and dividing!"

"Golly, *somebody* must have found a better way of doing it," Cathy said glumly, after trying every way she could think of.

"Not so fast! It took a long, long time to get to the number marks you people never wanted to see again," Mr. Dibbs reminded them.

"My brother is taking Geometry," Peggy said. "And he says the Greeks were great in mathematics. Maybe they had a better way of writing numbers. Did they, Mr. Dibbs?"

"Well," said Mr. Dibbs, "let's take a look at the way the Greeks wrote their numbers. They didn't invent new marks as the Egyptians did—the Greeks just used the letters of their alphabet."

"Say, that *was* smart," Peggy said.

"They called the *first* letter of their alphabet *alpha*," Mr. Dibbs said. "And it looked like this: a

"They let alpha be **1**

"The *second* letter is *beta*, and it looks like this: β

"Beta stood for **2**

"The *third* letter is *gamma*: V

"What do you think it stood for?"

"This is easy. Why don't we still do this?" Ralph asked.

"Let's go a little further," Mr. Dibbs said.

"Here are the first nine letters.

$$a \quad \beta \quad V \quad \delta \quad \epsilon \quad \varsigma \quad \varsigma \quad \eta \quad \theta$$
$$1 \quad 2 \quad 3 \quad 4 \quad 5 \quad 6 \quad 7 \quad 8 \quad 9$$

"Did they just let every letter represent a number?" Hallie asked. "How far could you go before you ran out of letters?"

"The Greeks were too smart to get stuck like *that*," Steve said. "They must have figured a way to use the rest of the letters to represent numbers above nine!"

"You're right," said Mr. Dibbs. "I'll show you what they did, but let's use our own alphabet instead of the Greek letters."

A	B	C	D	E	F	G	H	I
1	2	3	4	5	6	7	8	9

J	K	L	M	N	O	P	Q	R
10	20	30	40	50	60	70	80	90

S	T	U	V	W	X	Y	Z	*
100	200	300	400	500	600	700	800	900

"We ran out of letters, so we'll use a star for 900. Using this idea, how would you write **15**

This way   **JE**

How would you write
If the Greeks wrote this

to show how many boys were in swimming, how many boys *were* swimming?

"Say, Mr. Dibbs, this is just like a code," Joe laughed.

"Sure," said Mr. Dibbs. "But you have to know the rules for the code. Who has discovered a rule that the Greeks used?"

"The Greeks used the idea of addition when they wrote their numbers," Joe shouted.

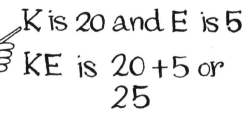

K is 20 and E is 5

KE is 20 + 5 or 25

Mr. Dibbs asked them if the Egyptians used this idea too. "*YES!*"

24

Peggy wrote

Mr. Dibbs said, "See what Joe wrote and what Peggy wrote? This gives you a clue to another rule the Greeks used."

Everybody looked blank.

"The Greeks could write their numbers without repeating number marks. Look again at how they both wrote 25."

"I told you the Greeks were smart," said Steve.

"Well, let's see how smart you are, Steve," Mr. Dibbs said. "Can you show us another rule the Greeks used so they did not have to repeat their symbols?"

Steve thought a minute, then shook his head.

"Sometimes," said Mr. Dibbs, "when you write an idea a little differently, it gives you more ideas. Here's just what we have been talking about, written in a different way.

Remember, we're using our alphabet because it's more familiar, but we're still talking about the Greek system.

25

		10 times	100 times
A	1	J (10×1)	S (100×1)
B	2	K (10×2)	T (100×2)
C	3	L (10×3)	U (100×3)
D	4	M (10×4)	V (100×4)
E	5	N (10×5)	W (100×5)
F	6	O (10×6)	X (100×6)
G	7	P (10×7)	Y (100×7)
H	8	Q (10×8)	Z (100×8)
I	9	R (10×9)	✳ (100×9)

"What do you notice when you look at it this way? They used a new number mark for

10 times any number up to 9

and 100 times any number up to 9

and of course they did something else for 1000 times any number up to 9, and so on."

M stood for 10 times what number? ↵

T stood for 100 times what number? ↵

What letter stood for 10 times 8? ↵

"Well, what's the catch?" Larry asked suspiciously. "Why don't we still use this system?"

26

"I'll bet that arithmetic would be hard with those letters," Candy said thoughtfully. "Let's try to add."

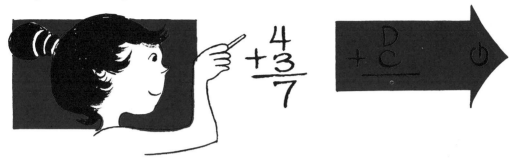

"That's crazy! $D + C = G$?"

"If you think that's crazy," Mr. Dibbs grinned, "what do you think $U + I =$?"

"Well, $U + I = UI$ isn't crazy at all," Peggy said. "That's easier than what we do now."

"Who would like to make one up for us?"

Danny jumped up. "I have a good one! What is

"I got yours, Danny," Larry shouted. "It's RG. Now let me give one!"

"I can't do it," Danny said. "But I could if I had more time."

27

"Well, while you're working on it, how about this subtraction example for everyone else." Mr. Dibbs wrote:

Candy groaned. "I can see the answer on that table," she said, "but I can't see any connection! If I wanted to subtract, I'd have to keep the table in front of me—it's like keeping the key to a code! But you couldn't always keep the code with you, and it would be awful to memorize."

Mr. Dibbs grinned and said, "And you thought *your* arithmetic was hard! For anybody who hasn't quit, here's another."

"All right," said Mr. Dibbs, who was now grinning from ear to ear. "Let's multiply. Or would you rather divide?"

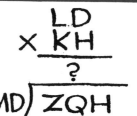

There was silence, then· many sighs.

Even Danny, who was still working, finally said, "I'm glad I wasn't born in those days! Homework must have taken forever."

"Okay, Mr. Dibbs," said David. "Let's have it. Who figured out a better way?"

"Well, the Romans were smart enough to conquer the world," Joe said. "I'll bet they were smart enough to figure out a better way to write numbers."

"Why, I've seen Roman numbers—we still use them for some things," Lisa said excitedly.

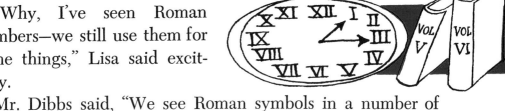

Mr. Dibbs said, "We see Roman symbols in a number of places. They look like this:

I V X L C D M

"Do any of you know what numbers these letters stand for?"

Everyone knew that

I is 1
V is 5
X is 10

Mr. Dibbs said,

"And L is 50
and C is 100

"I could guess that," said David. "It looks like the Egyptian mark for 100."

"Who can guess what these two letters stand for?" Mr. Dibbs asked. D M

"If you look at what we have written so far, you may see a pattern."

They all looked, and then Larry said, "I've got it!" He ran to the board and wrote

D is 500　M is 1000

"Why?" Mr. Dibbs asked.

"Well," Larry said,

V is 5 times the I
X is 2 times the V
L is 5 times the X
C is 2 times the L
D is 5 times the C
M is 2 times the D

"It wouldn't be hard to remember, if you just remembered 5 and 2 and 5 and 2."

"Now," Mr. Dibbs asked, "how do you think they wrote

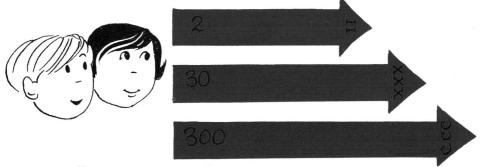

"Do you notice any rule that the Romans used in writing their numbers?"

"ADDITION!"

everybody said.

"Yes," Mr. Dibbs agreed, "*IF*. If the symbols are repeated, we add.

$$\underset{1+1}{\text{II}} \qquad \underset{10+10+10}{\text{XXX}} \qquad \underset{100+100+100}{\text{CCC}}$$

"But there's more to it than that.

"How did we write 10?"

Everybody said: "X, of course."

Mr. Dibbs grinned. "Why couldn't you write VV? Isn't VV 10?"

There was a dead silence, then Henry said, "Sure, VV is 10."

David said, "It is not! X is 10. Who ever saw VV?"

"Who's right, Mr. Dibbs?" Peggy asked.

"Before I answer," Mr. Dibbs said, "how would you write 100?"

Most people said C.

Henry said stubbornly, "I still think LL would be just as good."

"How about 1000?"

"*I'd* say M," David said.

"Well," said Henry, "*I'd* say DD!"

"There's a rule," said Mr. Dibbs. "We do not repeat

$$\text{V} \qquad \text{L} \qquad \text{D}$$

because of the way the Romans set up their number marks.

31

Remember?

> X equals twice V
>
> C equals twice L
>
> M equals twice D.

We never repeat V, L or D, because other letters mean double V, double L or double D."

How would you write

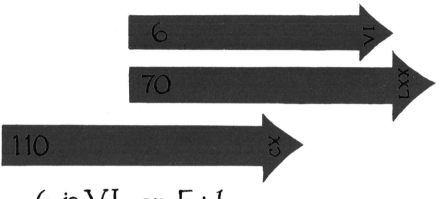

6 is VI or 5+1
70 is LXX or 50+10+10
110 is CX or 100+10

"What rule do you think we used here?"

"We're still adding," Lisa said.

"What else do you see?"

They thought for a minute, then Joe said, "The mark for the little number is always after the mark for the big number."

VI
LXX
CX

"Everybody agree?"

"It looks right," Laurie said. "But what happens if you put the smaller number first?"

"Gee, sometimes it *is* first," Joe said. "We have IV on our clock, and that means 4."

"Well, what does that tell you about how the Romans used their numbers?"

"That's easy! If the little number comes first, you subtract it from the big one. If it comes after, you add it," Laurie said excitedly.

"Now," said Mr. Dibbs. "How would you write

"Now write 49," said Mr. Dibbs, smiling. "But be careful— you still don't know *all* the rules."

"Wouldn't that be IL?" Larry asked.

"No it wouldn't. I told you you don't know all the rules."

"Gosh, the Romans were big on rules," said Henry gloomily.

33

Mr. Dibbs said,

"I, written to the left of V or X, shows that you are subtracting 1.

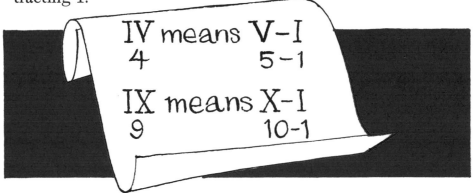

IV means V−I
4   5−1

IX means X−I
9   10−1

X, written to the left of L or C, shows that you are subtracting
10.

XL means L−X
50−10

XC means C−X
100−10

C, written to the left of D or M, shows that you are subtracting 100."

CD means D−C
500−100

CM means M−C
1000−100

Try these

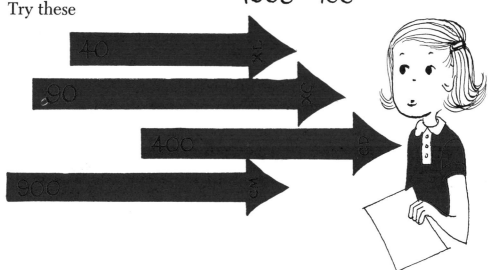

40   XL

90   XC

400   CD

900   CM

"By the way," Mr. Dibbs added, "I forgot to tell you part of the rule. You never put V, L or D in front of a letter of higher value, so if you want to write $\quad$ 45

you have to write $\quad$ X X X X V

not $\quad$ V L

How would you write

Henry said, "10 + 4 or XIV."

"But look!" Steve pointed. "You have two rules fighting each other! The I is after the X, so one rule says you add it. But it's in front of the V, so another rule says you subtract it! How do you know which to do?"

"They must have had *another* rule—that you subtract first, then add," Larry guessed.

"What's so great about the Roman system if you have to remember all those rules?" Joe asked. "How did they ever have *time* to conquer the world after they learned arithmetic?"

"Well," said Mr. Dibbs, "it *was* a good system, and people used it for a long time. Did you know that even when the colonists came to America, some children did their arithmetic with Roman number marks?"

35

"The kids must have been pretty smart in those days," Larry groaned.

Mr. Dibbs said cheerfully, "No smarter than you are.   It's very easy to add with these numbers.   Try this:

"See, you can add these numbers without knowing any number facts at all.   You just copy down all the marks!"

$$
\begin{array}{r}
XXII \\
+ \quad XI \\
\hline
XXXIII
\end{array}
$$

"Now try this one

"See how in the answer we replace the two V's with an X (remember the rule not to write VV), and the two L's with a C (remember, we can't write two L's).

Here are a few to try on your family."

$$
\begin{array}{r}
VI \\
+II \\
\hline
\end{array}
\qquad
\begin{array}{r}
XVII \\
+LXXXVI \\
\hline
\end{array}
\qquad
\begin{array}{r}
MDLXVII \\
+M \ XX \ III \\
\hline
\end{array}
$$

36

"You can subtract, too, without knowing number facts."
Try

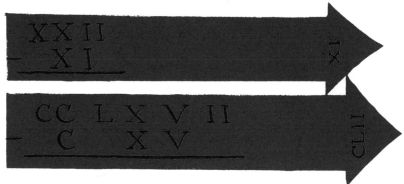

"This is the kind of arithmetic I like," said Cathy. "You don't have to know too much."

"Well, I'll bet multiplication and division are *awful,* or we'd all still be using the Roman system," Hallie said.

"You're right," said Mr. Dibbs. "How would you like to do these?

"But my conscience hurts a little," Mr. Dibbs said, "because I'm not exactly giving you *all* the facts. You couldn't do *written* arithmetic very well with this system, but
the Romans,
and people before them,
and many people since,
used a gadget we call an *abacus* to do their actual figuring.
"Wait a minute!"

Mr. Dibbs rummaged in the big desk drawer he called his treasure box, and pulled out a shell,

a harmonica,
and then——

"Behold an abacus," said Mr. Dibbs. "Later," he added mysteriously, "you *might* be able to figure out why everybody could work problems on this that were too complicated for number marks."

"Could we have time out for a meeting, Mr. Dibbs?" Arnold asked. The class whispered together while Mr. Dibbs looked out of the window and hummed to himself.

Then Arnold said, "Mr. Dibbs, I have been authorized by the class to *beg* for our numbers back."

Mr. Dibbs laughed. "Well, since you've worked your way through all those other systems, I guess you've earned them. But if I gave our numbers back to you the way they looked in the beginning, they might seem as strange as some of the others we've been working with."

He wrote on the board,

"These strange-looking numbers were first used by the Hindus, who passed them on to the Arabs. That's why, properly speaking, they are called Hindu-Arabic figures, and not just Arabic.

"This is the way they looked at about the time Columbus discovered America. The Roman number marks were still being used too, and for hundreds of years people argued which system was better."

"Why did they finally decide on ours?" Peggy asked.

"Well," Mr. Dibbs said, "there are two special ideas that none of those other systems had. Does anybody know what they are?

"I'll give you a clue. One was very, very simple, but sometimes the easiest ideas are the hardest to see.

"Look at this," Mr. Dibbs said, after a minute.

He wrote

	•	•	•	•	•	•	•	•	•	⋂ . . . . ⓒ
A	B	C	D	E	F	G	H	I	J . . . .
I	•	•	•	V	•	•	•	•	X L C D M
0	1	2	3	4	5	6	7	8	9	10 . . . 100 . . . . . .

"*ZERO!*" Henry shouted.

"Right! They never had a zero. That's what made so much of their arithmetic so hard. But zero alone isn't enough. Maybe this will give you a hint."

Mr. Dibbs wrote

fourteen
one hundred forty
four hundred one

"Now, write these in our number marks," he said.

14
140
401

"Does the *1* mean the same thing in each numeral?"
"Of course not," Cathy said.

40

"Let's try to figure out how this idea developed," Mr. Dibbs said, leaning against the wall and folding his hands on top of his head. "Imagine yourselves way back in time, and suppose you have a job counting the sacks of grain that are going to be a ship's cargo.

"To keep track of the sacks, you might match one sack to a finger until you had reached 10, and then make a pile out of those 10 sacks. Then you'd make another pile and another, until you had 10 piles of 10 sacks. Then you could put those 10 piles together into a superpile.

"Maybe when you finished counting your record would show that you had
1 superpile   3 piles of 10   and 2 sacks, all loaded on the ship. How many sacks would there be?"

132

"What does the 1 really show you?"

Steve said, "I superpile of 100! And the 3 would show me 3 piles of 10, and the 2 would show just 2 sacks."

"What if the clerk on another ship wrote

312

as a record of the sacks?" Mr. Dibbs asked. "The number marks are the same, but in a different order. Would the ships be carrying the same number of sacks?"

"Of course not!" Danny said. "This time,

the 3 means 3 superpiles of 100

the 1 means 1 pile of 10

the 2 means 2 sacks."

"Now you have the second important idea," Mr. Dibbs said. "Who knows what it is?"

"The values of the number marks depend on where you put them," David said. He wrote:

Superpiles 10 tens	piles tens	sacks ones
1	3	2
3	1	2

"Why, that's just like our place-value chart," said Peggy, in surprise.

Place value chart		
ten tens(100)	tens	ones
1	3	2
3	1	2

"What would the next place to the left be?" Mr. Dibbs asked.

"Well," David went on slowly, "each place has a value of 10 times the place to the right of it, so the next one has to be 10 times 100."

Place value chart			
ten hundreds(1000)	ten tens(100)	tens	ones
1	1 3	3 1	2 2

"Right!" said Mr. Dibbs. "Now what does 324 mean?

It means 3 hundreds + 2 tens + 4 ones

We can write

$$324 = 3 \times 100 + 2 \times 10 + 4 \times 1$$

"That looks long," Laurie said.

"Yes, it is," Mr. Dibbs agreed, "so we'll call it the long way of writing 324.

What would be the long way of writing

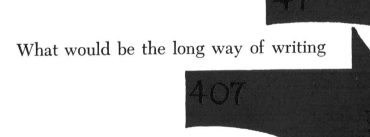

47

$4 \times 10 + 7 \times 1$

What would be the long way of writing

407

$4 \times 100 + 7 \times 1$

"The only difference in 47 and 407 is the zero."

"What a difference!" Joe said.

"In the long way of writing numbers," Mr. Dibbs went on, "you can see that we use the idea of addition, just as the Egyptians, the Greeks and the Romans did."

$$\text{C} + \cap = \text{C}\cap \quad \text{one hundred ten}$$
$$\text{S} + \text{J} = \text{SJ} \quad \text{one hundred ten}$$
$$\text{C} + \text{X} = \text{CX} \quad \text{one hundred ten}$$

one hundred + 1 ten = 110 one hundred ten
1 × 100 + 1 × 10

"But wait a minute," Steve said. "We use multiplication too! we multiply by 10
by 100
by 1000 and more!"

"Right!" said Mr. Dibbs. "Now let's stop and see what we've got.

"We have only 10 symbols. **0 1 2 3 4 5 6 7 8 9**
The Romans had fewer,
the Greeks had more,
but one of our symbols is zero.
the 10 symbols have two values each,

       face value   and   place value."

Mr. Dibbs wrote **22** on the board.
"The face value of each 2 is the same," he said. "But what is the place value of each 2? The place value of the 2 on the left is ten times the place value of the 2 on the right.

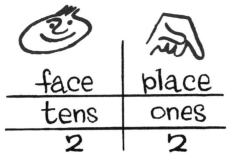

face	place
tens	ones
2	2

What is the face and place value of each 3 in 333?

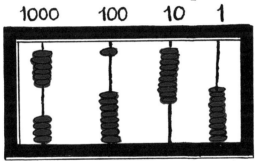

3 hundreds + 3 tens + 3 ones

"Incidentally," Mr. Dibbs said, holding up the abacus again. "That's why people could do arithmetic with an abacus when they couldn't do it with their written number marks. The beads on an abacus have place value.

1000   100   10   1

"You're lucky that place value is on your side," Mr. Dibbs said. "It makes it hard for you to make a mistake in arithmetic. In fact, it helps you to get the right answer in so many ways that you should hardly *ever* make a mistake!

"Look at this," Mr. Dibbs said.

He wrote   36   "84," Danny called out.
           +48   "How did you get 84, Danny?"

"I added 6 and 8, put down 4 and carried 1. Then 1, 3 and 4 are 8."

"Did anyone do it in a different way?" Mr. Dibbs asked. "No? Well, once I had a boy in my class who would add the 3 and 4 first, and then add the 6 and 8."

"That's crazy," said Steve.

"You bet," everyone agreed.

"Is it?" Mr. Dibbs laughed. "Not if you remember place value. Here are some of the ways I've seen boys and girls use it."

$$
\begin{array}{r} 36 \\ +48 \\ \hline 14 \\ 70 \\ \hline 84 \end{array}
\qquad
\begin{array}{r} 36 \\ +48 \\ \hline 14 \\ 7 \\ \hline 84 \end{array}
\qquad
\begin{array}{r} 36 \\ +48 \\ \hline 70 \\ 14 \\ \hline 84 \end{array}
\qquad
\begin{array}{r} 36 \\ +48 \\ \hline 7 \\ 14 \\ \hline 84 \end{array}
$$

"This is fun," Joe said. "You can find the answer in a lot of ways!"

"*If* you use what idea?"

"Place value!" everyone shouted.

"Place value helps you to add and subtract, multiply and divide," Mr. Dibbs said. "Try writing out these examples the long way, and you can see exactly what you're doing, even if you have never really thought about it before."

Addition

26   means 2 tens + 6 ones
+ 35   means 3 tens + 5 ones
_____
61   means 6 tens + 1 one

Subtraction

43   means 4 tens + 3 ones or 3 tens + 13 ones
− 26   means 2 tens + 6 ones or 2 tens + 6 ones
_____
17   1 ten + 7 ones

Multiplication

24   means 2 tens + 4 ones
× 3   × 3   × 3
_____
72   means   6 tens + 12 ones
                or 7 tens + 2 ones

Division

$$21 \div \quad \text{means} \quad 2\ tens + \quad 1\ one$$

$4\overline{)84}$ means $4\overline{)8\,tens} + 4\overline{)4\,ones}$

You can break down more difficult division problems like this:

$3\overline{)72}$ means } $3\overline{)7\,tens} + 3\overline{)2\,ones}$

$\dfrac{24}{3\overline{)72}}$ means }   OR

$3\overline{)6\,tens}^{\,2} + 3\overline{)12\,ones}^{\,4}$

Steve said, "I wonder what would happen if you worked some of those other number systems out the long way? Why don't we. . . ."

Just then the end-of-school bell rang.

"Oh, heck!" wailed Joe, "I wanted to write some of these out to try on my father! Can we go back to this the first thing tomorrow?"

Mr. Dibbs grinned, as he climbed up on his chair and started peeling the tape away from the face of the clock.